❦ History *of* Britain ❦

Victorian Railways

Andrew Langley

Illustrated by James Field

Heinemann

HISTORY OF BRITAIN – VICTORIAN RAILWAYS
was produced for Heinemann Children's Reference
by Lionheart Books, London

First published in Great Britain by Heinemann
Children's Reference, an imprint of Heinemann
Educational Publishers, a division of Reed
Educational and Professional Publishing Limited,
Halley Court, Jordan Hill, Oxford OX2 8EJ

MADRID ATHENS
FLORENCE PRAGUE WARSAW
PORTSMOUTH NH CHICAGO SAO PAULO MEXICO
SINGAPORE TOKYO MELBOURNE AUCKLAND
IBADAN GABORONE JOHANNESBURG KAMPALA NAIROBI

© Reed Educational & Professional Publishing Ltd 1996

Editors: Lionel Bender, Sue Reid
Designer: Ben White
Editorial Assistant: Madeleine Samuel
Picture Researcher: Jennie Karrach
Media Conversion: Peter MacDonald
Typesetting: R & B Partnership

Educational Consultant: Jane Shuter
Editorial Advisors: Andrew Farrow, Paul Shuter
Production Controller: David Lawrence
Editorial Director: David Riley

ISBN 0 600 58839 4 Pb
ISBN 0 600 58838 6 Hb

British Library Cataloguing-in-Publication Data.
A catalogue record for this book is available from
the British Library.

Printed in Italy

Acknowledgements
The Publishers would like to thank the following for permission
to reproduce photographs.

NRM = National Railway Museum, York. SM = The Science Museum,
London. SSPL = Science & Society Picture Library.
l = left, r = right, t = top, b = bottom, c = centre.

Pages: 4, 5t: SM/SSPL. 5c: The Mansell Collection. 5b: Fotomas Index. 6t:
The Mansell Collection. 7bl: The Royal Museum & Art Gallery, Canterbury,
Kent. 6-7b: NRM/SSPL. 7cr: The Mansell Collection. 8l: NRM/SSPL. 8r:
Fotomas Index. 9t: SM/SSPL. 9b: NRM/SSPL. 10: SM/SSPL. 11t:
NRM/SSPL. 11b: SM/SSPL. 12t: Museum of London. 12b: Elton
Collection/Ironbridge Gorge Museum Trust. 13t: NRM. 13c: Hulton Deutsch
Collection. 14t: Robert Opie. 15t: NRM/SSPL. 15c: Bridgeman Art
Library/Birmingham Museum & Art Gallery. 15b: Hulton Deutsch Collection.
16tr: Thomas Cook Travel Archive. 16tl, 17tl: NRM/SSPL. 16b, 17b:
Hulton Deutsch Collection. 18t: National Postal Museum. 18b: Robert Opie.
19c: SM/SSPL. 19b: Hulton Deutsch Collection. 20b: Popperfoto. 21tl:
NRM. 21tr: Robert Harding Picture Library/Christopher Nicholson. 21b:
Hulton Deutsch Collection. 22t: The Mansell Collection. 22c: Hulton
Deutsch Collection. 22b: Robert Harding Picture Library.
Cover: Illustration by James Field, Survey map and Passenger painting
(NRM/SSPL), Portrait of train accident victim (Mansell Collection), Railway
tickets (Robert Opie)
All illustrations by James Field except maps, by Hayward Art Group.
Every effort has been made to contact copyright holders of any material
reproduced in this book. Any omissions or errors will be rectified in subse-
quent printings if notice is given to the Publisher.

PLACES TO VISIT

Here are some museums, preserved lines and sites of railway interest to visit. There are dozens more: your local tourist office can tell you about other places in your area. If there is any kind of railway near you, it is also worth studying for clues to its Victorian past.

Bala Lake Railway, Gwynedd. Steam trips through dramatic lakeside scenery.

Bluebell Line, Horsted Keynes, Sussex. A working railway with many steam locomotives.

Bo'ness and Kinneil Railway, West Lothian. Scotland's biggest collection of steam locomotives.

Bowes Railway Centre, Tyne and Wear. Built by George Stephenson, this is Britain's only rope-hauled railway.

Colne Valley Railway, Essex. Fine collection of old railway buildings and rolling stock.

Darlington Railway Centre and Museum, Darlington. Built in 1842, the station contains – among many other exhibits – George Stephenson's original 'Locomotion'.

Didcot Railway Centre, Oxfordshire. Concentrates on Brunel's Great Western Railway (GWR). A reconstructed section of broad-gauge line is one of many exciting features.

Ffestiniog Railway, Gwynnedd. The most famous preserved narrow-gauge line, dating from the 1830s.

Isle of Wight Steam Railway. Several Victorian locomotives amongst the rolling stock.

Keighley and Worth Valley Railway, Keighley, Yorkshire. Preserved line featured in the film *The Railway Children*.

National Railway Museum, York. A massive collection of old stock, including royal trains and a replica of 'Rocket'.

North Yorkshire Moors Railway, Pickering. Scenic route originally built by George Stephenson.

Science Museum, London. Includes many relics from the early years of railway transport.

South Devon Railway, Buckfastleigh. Steam trips in a vivid Great Western atmosphere.

Ulster Folk and Transport Museum, County Down. Among many exhibits is the largest locomotive ever built in Ireland.

INTRODUCTION

The industrial revolution of the eighteenth century depended on two vital materials – coal and iron. Vast amounts of these minerals had to be carried from mines to factories and foundries. But how? Roads were muddy and rutted, and a horsedrawn wagon could not carry much.

The first answer to the problem was canals. The boats, also hauled by horses, could transport far greater weights of raw materials. Many new canals were dug. But even these could not meet the growing demand.

Clearly, horse muscle was no longer enough. Early in Queen Victoria's reign, it was replaced by a much more powerful force – steam. Steam locomotives could pull far bigger loads over far greater distances. The Railway Age had begun.

CONTENTS

STEAM ON THE MOVE

Steam power had been in use since the early 1700s. The early beam engines pumped water out of coal mines. During the 1760s, James Watt developed better engines that could power spinning machines and looms, and turn factory lathes and drills.

Railways were much older. Wagons, drawn by horses along wooden rails (wagonways), had been used in European mines since the Middle Ages. In 1767, the first iron rails were laid in Britain at Coalbrookdale iron-smelting works in Shropshire. Later, wagons were fitted with iron wheels, which made them run more freely. But early steam engines were too heavy to propel themselves along. It was not until 1804 that Richard Trevithick built the first successful steam locomotive.

△ **This wooden wagonway** was built at Bath in 1731 to move stone from the nearby quarries to build the city's elegant houses.

▷ **Robert Stephenson's locomotive 'Rocket'** at the Rainhill Trials of 1829.

◁ **One of Richard Trevithick's early steam locomotives.** They were so heavy that they broke both wooden and cast-iron rails.

▽ **Locomotives at the Rainhill Trials of 1829.** The builders of the Liverpool and Manchester Railway held the trials to decide which had the most reliable design. Five locomotives took part. The winner was the 'Rocket', built by Stephenson's son Robert.

△ **A list of the rivals in the Rainhill Trials.** 'Novelty' blew up, 'Sans Pareil' broke down, and neither 'Cycloped' nor 'Perseverance' reached the required speed.

One man saw clearly that steam railways had a big future. George Stephenson, born to a poor Newcastle family, devoted himself to designing a locomotive which was reliable, strong and not too massive. In 1814, his first engine pulled 30 tonnes of coal along rails at Killingworth.

Soon afterwards, Stephenson launched a much bigger project – the building of a railway to carry coal from the Durham pits to the port of Stockton, 43 kilometres away.

The Stockton and Darlington Railway opened in September 1825, its first train of 38 wagons and nearly 600 passengers hauled by Stephenson's 'Locomotion No.1'.

Though most of the line's trains were later horse-drawn, it was a huge success. Within 18 months, the cost of producing coal in Stockton had fallen by half. But already a new and even larger railway line was being constructed, linking Manchester and the port of Liverpool.

RAILWAY MANIA BEGINS

On 15 September 1830, the Liverpool and Manchester Railway (LMR) was opened. Thousands of people watched as eight special trains puffed by, carrying important guests. They also witnessed the first fatal railway accident.

▷ **Robert Stephenson's 'Planet'** waits to start the 7 am service on the LMR. The line was a triumph of engineering. It went over the huge bog of Chat Moss, and through a rock cutting, 21 metres deep. Finally, it crossed a huge nine-arch viaduct.

△ **The sad fate of a Midlands stagecoach.** By the 1840s, the great days of stagecoach travel were over.

▽ **The grand opening of the Canterbury and Whitstable Railway in May 1830.** Only a short section of the line was worked by steam locomotive.

Despite this tragedy, the new line quickly became popular. It was the first steam passenger railway, with trains travelling twice as fast as a stagecoach. Within eighteen months, it had carried over 700,000 people, and was showing a profit. Gradually, businessmen realized that railways could make a lot of money. They were keen to invest in railway schemes.

Each new scheme had to be approved by an Act of Parliament. Between 1833 and 1836, permission was given for four major lines. Three connected London with Birmingham, Southampton and Bristol. The fourth linked Birmingham with the Liverpool and Manchester Railway.

The success of the early lines inspired others. By 1836, the first bout of 'railway mania' was gripping the country. New railway companies sprang up. They encouraged people to buy shares in their schemes, promising huge profits.

By 1838, Parliament had given permission for over 2,400 kilometres of new lines. These spread the rail network out to Exeter in the west, Yarmouth in the east and Dundee in the north.

▷ **Liverpool MP William Huskisson**, who fell in front of the 'Rocket' and was crushed to death at the opening of the LMR.

▽ **A first-class passenger and mail train on the LMR.** The guard sits on top of the front carriage. A coach is carried at the rear.

THE MAIN LINES 1837-1850

The web of railways spread rapidly. Britain's major cities and ports were joined by main, or trunk, lines. Robert Stephenson built the link from London to Birmingham. Joseph Locke took charge of the Grand Junction between Birmingham and Liverpool.

▷ **The great railway engineers**, Robert Stephenson (left) and Isambard Kingdom Brunel (right), watch the launching of Brunel's giant steamship, the *Great Eastern*, in 1858.

△ **Fashionable ladies wait for their train** at Euston Station in 1837, the year it opened. It was London's first main line railway terminus, and attracted many sightseers. A London footman wrote of the new station: "The steam engine is something like a very large barrel on four wheels. It's wonderful how such a small thing can drag so many coaches after it with such a weight."

But the most colourful railway engineer of all was Isambard Kingdom Brunel. Brilliant and ruthless, he had a hand in building every part of the Great Western Railway from Paddington Station in London to the West Country. This was begun in 1835 and reached Bristol in 1841.

Brunel surveyed the route and bargained with landowners to cross their property. One was paid £7,500 (about £ ¾ million at today's values); another complained that the line would ruin his fishpond (Brunel wrote: "I will make him a dozen fishponds for the same money.").

Besides this, Brunel designed station buildings, carriages, tunnels and bridges. He hired contractors to carry out the building work and inspected it regularly. He invented an 'atmospheric' railway which ran on vacuum suction (though this was a failure). He even built huge steamships to carry passengers from Bristol across the Atlantic Ocean. It is not surprising that he, like Stephenson and Locke, died from stress and strain of work in his early fifties.

△ **The railway works at Swindon on the GWR.**
Newly built engines are moved along the tracks (centre).
The lines are Brunel's 'broad gauge' (2.1 metres wide
instead of the standard 1.3 ˚metres).

Parliament was worried that the growth
of railways was out of control. In 1844,
Trade Minister William Gladstone set
out new rules for the railway companies.
He also forced them to run one
train each day at a cheap rate.
All the same, a new bout of
'railway mania' broke out in
1845. Over the next three
years, Parliament gave
approval for over 13,500
kilometres of new lines
(though only about 4,800
were ever built).

◁ **Railway surveyors
(far left) check the
level of a new stretch
of track.** Surveyors also
planned the line using a
local map (left). They
had to choose between
the shortest route (which
might require expensive
bridges or tunnels) and
the cheapest (which
might be far longer).

NAVVIES AT WORK

"All the roads and lanes are overrun with drunken navvies... I have not in my travels seen anything uglier than that mass of labourers." This is how writer Thomas Carlyle saw the 'navvies' who did the dirty work of building the railways. In 1846, there were over 200,000 of them throughout Britain.

The navvies moved across the country in vast armies as the railways advanced. They lived in shanty towns built of mud and wood. But they were well-paid, earning twice as much as a farm labourer. On paydays, they were often drunk and eager to fight.

Navvies worked very hard. There were no machines to help them as they dug cuttings and tunnels, raised embankments and built bridges. Their only tools were picks, shovels and wheelbarrows, with gunpowder to blast away the hardest rock. A good navvy could shift 20 tonnes of rubble in a day.

▽ **Navvies using horse runs** to move earth at Tring Cutting in Hertfordshire in 1837.

▽ (Far below) **Navvies hard at work** on a cutting in the early 1840s. They fill their barrows with rubble, then push them up narrow plank 'runs'. Others are building the wooden frame for the arches of a bridge. A train of wagons on a temporary track brings materials and carries away more rubble.

10

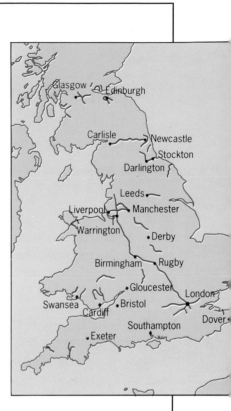

◁ **Navvies splitting rocks by hand** to build a railway tunnel in about 1845. ('Navvy' is short for navigators.) Many of these men were from Ireland, where there were few jobs to be had.

▷ **The railway network in 1838.** A web of lines stretched out from London, Manchester, Newcastle and Edinburgh, and a continuous line ran from London to Liverpool.

We take railways for granted. It is easy to forget the gigantic effort needed to build them. Unlike roads, railways had to be as flat and straight as possible. Hollows were filled in and valleys crossed with bridges. Hills caused greater problems and had to be cut or tunnelled through.

Many navvies were killed, especially during the dangerous work of tunnelling. Danger came from rock and mud falls, poisonous fumes and dust in the air, careless lighting of gunpowder, and flooding. At Woodhead Tunnel in Cheshire, completed in 1845, 32 navvies died in accidents, and dozens more of disease. Over 100 men lost their lives digging Box Tunnel, in Wiltshire.

◁ **The digging of Kilsby Tunnel** on the London and Birmingham Railway in 1837. Navvies and equipment were lowered into the tunnel through a work shaft, as here. After work began, water flooded in from a spring; it took eight months to pump the water out.

11

BUILDING BRIDGES

The most thrilling pieces of railway engineering were the bridges and viaducts. They strode across valleys and rivers, and were the biggest structures many Victorians had ever seen. Early bridges were built of brick or timber, later ones of iron or steel.

△ **A commemorative railway medal.**

▷ **Robert Stephenson's Britannia Bridge** being built over the Menai Straits in 1849. The first iron tube has already been fixed. The second is being floated out on two pontoons. When it is in the correct place, the pontoons will be filled with water and slightly sunk, letting the tube rest on timber piles at each end. It will then be raised up into position by hydraulic lifts.

The first of the great railway bridges crossed the Menai Straits, a distance of 330 metres. It was designed by Robert Stephenson, who seemed to have an impossible problem. His bridge must not get in the way of Royal Navy ships in the Straits, so could not have low arches. He solved this by building three towers (one on a rock in mid-stream) and spanning them with two massive wrought-iron tubes, or girders. Each was 140 metres long: until then, the biggest girder bridge had been only 18 metres.

Brunel had similar trouble in 1853 when he planned to bridge the Tamar River at Saltash, near Plymouth. The width was as great, and once again the Royal Navy would not allow any arches to obstruct their ships. Worse still, there was no rock in the middle on which to build a tower. Brunel had to sink a great iron tube through 24 metres of water and mud, and then pump out the water before he could build his central pier. The bridge itself was held taut by two arched tubes. Trains still travel across it today.

▷ **Painters put the finishing touches to the Royal Albert Bridge** at Saltash, between Devon and Cornwall. Down below are the old naval ships used to transport the wrought iron. In 1859, Brunel went to see the opening of the bridge, but was too ill to stand. He was laid on a couch and pulled slowly across the bridge on a truck. He died only four months later. Altogether, Brunel's railway in Cornwall had to cross eight estuaries and 34 deep valleys. To save money, he built viaducts of timber on stone piers.

◁ **The bridge carrying the railway over the River Thames** to Charing Cross Station in London. Signals and a signal box are built over the tracks.

Not everyone was so successful. In 1878, Thomas Bouch completed his bridge across the Firth of Tay in Scotland. But 18 months later, the bridge collapsed, plunging a train and passengers into the water below. Bouch also worked on a bridge across the Firth of Forth. The Tay disaster ruined him, and a new designer was hired. The result was the first all-steel bridge, opened in 1890.

△ **The Forth Bridge takes shape.** Opened in 1890, it was over 2.4 kilometres long. It was built on the cantilever principle, which the designer compared to two men trying to shake hands across a stream: "one man extends his walking stick, and the other grasps it".

TRAVELLING BY TRAIN

From the start, there were three classes of carriage. The most expensive and luxurious was first class. The cheapest was third class, where passengers had to sit on draughty plank seats. However, by 1860, there were more third-class passengers than first and second combined.

▷ **Tickets issued by the Great Western Railway Company** for journeys from Weymouth Station in Dorset. The ticket clerk would write in the date, destination and fare.

Even a small station had a large staff, including a porter, ticket clerk, signalman and the station-master himself. Local farmers would bring milk churns and goods to the station for transport by train.

▽ **A country station in the 1880s.** Passengers wait on the platform to board their train.

14

◁ **Abraham Solomon's** *The Meeting* shows the plush and roomy comforts of a first-class carriage.

◁ **Sleeping or reading** – two ways of passing the time on a train journey – shown in Augustus Egg's *Travelling Companions* (below left).

Even for first-class passengers on main lines, a railway journey in the 1860s could be uncomfortable. In winter, the unheated carriages were very cold. The only heat came from metal 'foot-warmers' filled with hot water. (Third-class passengers only got these in 1873!) There were no corridors and no toilets.

Travellers must have been very glad to stop at a station, not only to relieve themselves but also to buy food. Even this became more difficult. Railways were anxious to run faster services and cut the waiting time in stations. The first restaurant car only appeared in 1874.

The lack of corridors was even more alarming. Passengers could not move from their compartment, even in an emergency. Several were attacked by robbers or drunkards, and some even murdered. In 1868 'communication cords' were rigged outside carriages to raise the alarm. These were fixed to a whistle or bell on the engine. Corridor trains began running in 1892.

▽ **Dover Priory Station in 1886.** To the left are goods trucks which would have been loaded by crane. In the centre, a main line locomotive pulls a passenger train from the shed. Shunting locomotives wait in the sidings on the right.

TRAINS AND TRADE

"Here lies a waggonload of beer from Chester, there another of sugar-loaves from Northampton...." This description of a London goods yard was written in the late 1840s and shows that huge variety of mixed goods were carried on the railways.

By far the biggest and most important cargo was coal. It was vital not only as a fuel for factories and iron foundries, but also to produce gas for street lighting. The first railways had, of course, been built just to transport coal. After 1850, it made up half of all the freight carried by rail. Over 7 million tonnes went to London alone.

The building of the railways also helped to expand trade in many other products. 'Perishables' (fresh foods) such as milk, fruit and fish could be taken speedily from farms and ports to city centres. Bulky and heavy raw materials, such as Cornish china clay or iron ore, could be moved cheaply to industrial areas. At the docks, freight could be loaded from ships directly on to trains.

△ **Letters postmarked on mail trains** in 1860 and 1884. 'Night Down' was an overnight train to London. Payment of a 'Late fee' by the sender ensured next morning delivery.

▷ **Letters and parcels being sorted** by postal workers in a mail coach on the move. People could hand in mail at the coach until a few minutes before the train was due to leave.

▷ **Part of a Victorian poster** for Great Northern Railway (GNR), advertising transport of luggage and mail by trains from King's Cross Station in London. The net structure on the side of the carriage scooped up mail bags that were suspended from poles alongside the track without the train stopping.

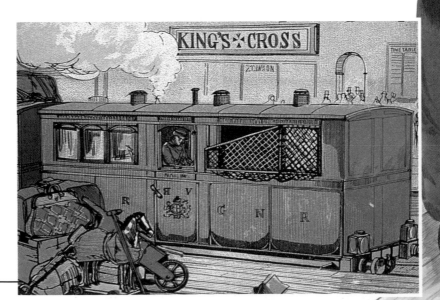

Trains also carried news. The Post Office had sent mail by train as early as 1830. This was an important step, for it showed that railways were thought reliable and safe. By 1838, letters were being sorted on the move in special carriages called mail coaches. By the 1880s everything from newspapers to cattle was being transported by train.

By making fast, cheap connections between distant parts of Britain, railways encouraged new industries and towns to grow. Factories no longer had to be near a source of raw materials. Workers no longer had to live within walking distance of their workplace.

△ **Colliery pit-head and railway yard at Burton on Trent.** Coal was also vital as fuel for steam locomotives.

◁ **Wagons at a slate quarry** in Llanberis, North Wales in about 1880. The line is built to a narrow gauge, with only 0.6 metres between the two rails.

RED FOR DANGER

Early trains were dangerous. Locomotive boilers might blow up. People on the ground, unused to the speed of a steam engine, might be run down. Trains might crash into each other. To stop this happening, a system of signals was slowly developed.

▽ **The Great Western locomotive 'Sultan' gets up steam** ready for a day's work in the 1870s.

▽ (Far below) **The guard signals his commuter train** is about to leave a London station in 1885.

Locomotive safety features from about 1870

▷ **Head and tail lamps** help train crews and track workers see other trains.

▷ **A steam valve** (small funnel) allows excess steam to escape from the boiler. **A steam whistle** was used to signal the train's arrival or departure.

△ **Buffers** front and back cushioned any impact.

△ **Sand stored in boxes** was released on to the track from pipes to give the wheels extra grip on hills or when pulling heavy loads.

△ **An engineer** checked wheels for cracks by tapping them with an iron hammer.

The first railway signals were human. Men stood at intervals along the track, and used flags or their hands to tell drivers to stop, slow down or carry on. Simple mechanical signals appeared in 1834. These were red boards which were turned to face the driver as a warning.

Signalling was made much easier by the invention of the telegraph in the late 1830s. Signalmen were now able to send messages to each other about train times over long distances.

△ **Signalmen pose outside the signalbox** at Moortown in Lincolnshire.

△ **A driver's eye view.** The footplate of a Great Western Railway steam locomotive still in use today.

▽ **A train crash** near Clapham Junction in 1868.

△ **The crew** had little shelter from weather and coal smoke. **The guard** had a seat at the back (above right).

By the 1840s, groups of signals were controlled by one man in a signalbox. But efficient signals were no use unless the trains had efficient brakes. For years, railway companies were too mean to fit them. It took a horrific crash in Armagh in 1889 for Parliament to make automatic brakes compulsory.

THE RAILWAY AGE

When Victoria became queen in 1837, there were about 2,300 kilometres of railway track in Britain. When she died in 1901, there were 30,000 kilometres. Railways carried over 1,000 million passengers a year, and had an income of £100 million.

"The railways are the wonder of the age", wrote a poet. They had changed the face of town and country and made people more mobile than ever before.

Trains were also the fastest machines ever built. Stephenson's 'Rocket' could travel at 60 km/h. In 1904, a Great Western train reached 160 km/h.

▷ **The opening of the first railway in Japan**, in 1872. This sketch of a station and signal box was made by a Japanese artist. The buildings look very European. All Japanese railway lines were built to a narrow gauge.

▷ **Excited crowds watch** as the first train puffs proudly out of Rangoon, Burma. The Rangoon and Irrawaddy State Railway was opened in 1877. Burma was then under British rule. The British built railways in many of their colonies, notably India. Here, over 39,000 kilometres of line were completed by 1900.

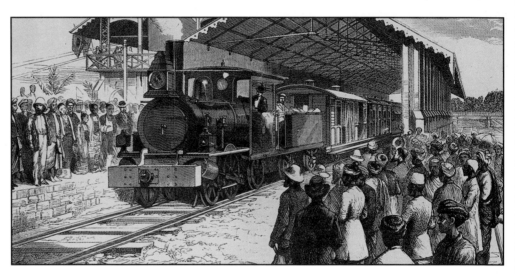

British engineers helped to spread railways to Europe and beyond. Robert Stephenson sold locomotives to Austria and Germany. British contractors and navvies also took their skills abroad.

Tracks soon crossed entire continents. In 1869, the coast-to-coast Union Pacific Railroad was built in the USA. By 1900, a single line linked Moscow with Siberia. The railway had conquered the world.

▷ **The signalman's view of a steam train on the Pickering and North Yorkshire Railway.** This is one of many lines built in Victorian times which have been preserved all over Britain. Visitors can relive the thrill of riding behind a steam locomotive.

GLOSSARY

beam engine steam engine which rocks a beam up and down; this creates the vacuum for pumping.

cantilever a bracket or block which supports a beam.

cast iron piece made by pouring molten iron into a mould.

contractor person hired to build something or supply materials.

footplate platform for train driver and assistant on steam locomotive.

foundry place where iron is melted, refined and cast.

freight goods carried by train or by other forms of transport.

gauge measurement between the two rails.

girder a horizontal beam of metal or timber which supports a weight.

hydraulic a system of operating a machine by using water under pressure.

iron ore iron as it is mined, mixed with other minerals and impurities.

locomotive an engine which can push itself along.

navvy a labourer originally hired to dig ('navigate') canals.

pontoon a large, flat-bottomed boat.

rolling stock the engine and vehicles that run upon a railway.

shares a part of the value of a company, which can be bought; a 'shareholder' expects to be paid out of the profits of the company.

stagecoach a four-wheeled horse-drawn coach which carried passengers and mail between 'stages', or parts of a journey.

telegraph a system for sending messages by using electric impulses.

terminus the station at the end of a railway line.

viaduct a series of arches carrying a road or railway over a valley.

wrought iron iron which is shaped by hammering or rolling.

▽ **The Victorian railway network**
showing the major lines and city interchanges that were completed by 1838, 1851 and about 1895.

The Railway Network 1838

The Railway Network 1851

The Railway Network 1890s

TIMECHART

1767 First iron railway built at Coalbrookdale.

1804 Trevithick builds first successful steam locomotive.

1825 Stockton and Darlington Railway opens.

1829 Robert Stephenson's 'Rocket' wins Rainhill Trials.

1830 Liverpool and Manchester Railway opens.

1836 First bout of 'railway mania' begins.

1837 London and Birmingham Railway opens.

1838 First mail sorting coaches.

1841 Great Western Railway reaches Bristol.

1844 Act of Parliament regulates how railway companies operate.

1845 Second bout of 'railway mania'.

1850 Stephenson's Britannia Bridge completed.

1859 Brunel's Royal Albert Bridge completed.

1863 First line on London's Underground Railway opens.

1874 First restaurant car runs on Midland Railway.

1879 Tay Bridge collapses in a storm.

1890 Forth Bridge opens.

1892 Corridor trains begin running on the GWR.

INDEX